Conjugation

Phil Hall · Conjugation

BookThug

FIRST EDITION

Cover and interior by Beautiful Outlaw
Copy edited by Ruth Zuchter

WWW.BOOKTHUG.CA

The production of this book was made possible through the generous assistance of the Canada Council for the
Arts and the Ontario Arts Council. BookThug also acknowledges the support of the Government of Canada
through the Canada Book Fund and the Government of Ontario through the Ontario Book Publishing Tax Credit
and the Ontario Book Fund.

LIBRARY AND ARCHIVES CANADA CATALOGUING IN PUBLICATION

Hall, Phil, 1953–
        Conjugation / Phil Hall.
Poems.

Issued in print and electronic formats.
PAPERBACK: ISBN 978-1-77166-218-5
HTML: ISBN 978-1-77166-219-2
PDF: ISBN 978-1-77166-220-8
MOBI: ISBN 978-1-77166-221-5

        I. Title.

PS8565.A449C66 2016   C811'.54   C2015-908754-6 | C2015-908755-4

PRINTED IN CANADA

Contents

The Stile

These fields   picked-clear   hoof & rut   sown   for grazing
make a peace   by collapse   with the clenched   woodlots

driving alone   to ruminate   on highlands   & settlements

I venerate   bog geometry   each slumped   compromise
I pull over   & wade out   into corn stubble   mud rows

blue thistle   bull thistle   here a box-stove door   still readable

where scrub-cedars   burst   to retake   hard-won   fallow
I pet   fuzzled   royal mould   on split-rails   gone spongy

in the shaking   amanita caves   of the high pasture   butternuts

on land   owned   but almost   not owned
a border   forgotten   vouches for me   & I climb   over

my baby toes have only claws   to be ignored is my legitimacy

I am a stagnant churning   high & brief
all is tough-titty   mulch   & shade

I · Gap & Hum

Early *ideot amonug*
fog litfs   spelling improves

foraging along   the sh

between words   old eurekas
cadential dromenon

~

Vacant   lug-nutted   the striped lots

full *stadiums waving   bellowing*
equal   incipit   this page   founded

on shush   foundered   by a few tiny

arcs   letters   *curls of let*
wait wit   wait   a song   grows a nail

from a moo/   a mo/

~

Early   can still catch   out   writing at its oldest posture
to set down care alone   & quiet matters   personal defiant fleet·

to dare from self-loathing   the eternal   & then erase it

I want little more   *have always wanted   the littles   more*
now than   another morning to say   what's been said   already

another morning   to waste   figuring out   uselessly   how to

stick in somewhere here   *screws for dragonfly lights*   (a note I found)
I want this in my poem   is all   & ruin at bay   for my loved ones

~

Awake before daylight
out back   again   blind listening

past the wet grass   that black clump is trees

in the swamp   the peepers
have turned their little   slime Singers   up again

treadle   peg & awl   treadle   peg & awl

praise & desperation   aim & itch   a 1-on-1
row-yr-boat   that wins   & wins   & wins

at nothing   possible   any syllable   repeated   now

can seem like   what them new frogs   are trying
to translate   another undo-able brevet   from Lao Tzu

sew dew, eye   so do I   sew dew-eye   so, do I?

~

This morning   I couldn't sleep
& was up too early   binning the ashes

when I grated against   the black horse   again

a muzzle-hair / quill   a tar-dipped   brush-tip
its sway   unwelted   by any saddle

night   nigh   steam-close   quivering

not a horse   a horse-wolverine
a panther-moose   *a lamprey*

inside me   I would ride   yet hide

most mornings   I am almost   on it   or off it
as grey light comes over the trees

no   first greyness   suggests   tree-ness

then grey light   *suggestifies*   pines
then daylight   *specifies*   white pine

~

Bay-by-bay   gung-ho

mufflers   trace   the lake
& now our freight-local

shunts its fool   sepia   through town

insects in the   *in the   in the*
where wet nests   a dank under-rush

this pencil scritching along

a voice dressing up as a cricket
an equivocation   in nor out

a finding of   *go-stays*

13

~

Wake up   *creased sharp*   take a pill
a remember when   old drinking-wound   my ribs

in our bay   the lake frozen   12" thick

& gauzed   at dawn   by more fresh   night-snow
a deer has stepped   from the island   to our dock

& back   almost in the same   split   hoof-holes

out past where   ice-fishing wells   might augur
a perforated line   pricks light   grey-green   black

roust new   cross a page again   *untorn*   *unfolded*

~

Orange chair   blue porch   white Stetson
am re-reading   *Cold Mountain*   translated by Red Pine

woke to fog   a cremation dream   it is garbage day

Olson: *words made to taste*   *like accuracy*   *pincers*
the king birds are back   an osprey shrieks

in the wooded swamp   ice reigns yet   first the school bus

no motor   no driver   passes   only one child so far   up front
then the Trueloves   would it hurt them to signal   bastards

despair is elitist   do not count pages   forget   *the work*

w & k   both built   from 2 *V*s   or 3   end up with only   *or*
deface the cartoon   until the joke   is fearful

14

~

Sh   that horse head   nailed   above the archway
recites   its old riddles   to me   only now   early

under   my cheap lamp's   shade   a hum   dust

these *madrugar*   I've written of late   feel raw   briary
leprechaun-ish   a few yammer   loony-zoned   like Mr Ed

the talking horse   or remember Francis   the army mule

who only talked   w w i i vaudeville   to Donald O'Connor   *who?*
the Wheel-Trans drivers   will soon be up   the school buses

idling   their manifolds   & cabs warmed   just enough

baby bottles   knocking in pans   on stoves   5:17   *blur* a m
Je mets tout de ma vie, j'adore ça.

Baiser la nuit, son bord, c'est ma cuisine. (Marie Étienne)

me   I'm tired   of listening   to everything   that once   spoke
nonsense   other-true   *help!*   again white   establishes light

as the list-all   & straighten-all   *protect us!*   Saint Syntax   pulls

the usual   stale treats   from his robe   *predicate / modifier*
bribes   in each line   b-right logic   a silencing   *sh*

~

At the extremity   of this design
privilege   is misspelled   no it's not   *noit's not*

~

A first draft   blind in its pride
snubs the glistening crossroads of its foliage

we were tightened   by a primmer   under-alphabet

how-to-behave   nodding along   to the 1%
milk-of-human-kindness   white baton

~

16   I have   at last   no face   for fact

but there's a fee
a fee that sees   & hears wonky

fe-ces   we're were   subtler / fugues   etc

until I get scared   & take it all back   too far
ashamed of play's ruthlessness

biting my lip   green dawn   akimbo

~

Equitable hodge   ego rip
another   Little Square-One   ready to send out

stinking   of metaphor

noise that says   *I am edible   because I hunger*
from *gnat*   to *natter*   the mouth   healing shut

its words   fallen back   into it

the lake   over the leap   17
to not take the bait   the beat

~

In the morning   the poem solves everything

in the afternoon   it stinks   & I stink too
the little structural satisfactions   have to be broken

so   the trite suck   of my ego   at play   in a line

is exposed   for the pander   & cop-out   it tries
but if the poem works   in defiance of me   I can't explain   how

by pointing at anything   about myself   or what I studied

posit no   *archeological fallacy*
chuck the vinyl

~

Watching   from above the depot   the faces

of those   who have just gotten off   who are being met
the stinking dock   sloshing

they loosen   they risk anticipation   *hey*

& the faces   of those who have been waiting   take a risk too
hey   but to see both risks   you have to be still on the train

almost underway   looking down   as if not there   drama-less

a lifeguard   a goddess
any fool   can draw the ocean   icon   & get for it

tickets   to the Sympathy   tear them up

crowbar loose the curled shingles   throw yr sheep
yr metaphors   into the chop

force subtlety   its cold eye

~

What the dot   above the *i*   is called

Hugh knows   it's a *tittle*   a kinetic speck
say *fish* & big-mouthed   itself tittled   the word leaps

up   out   at   other little words of ours   *is   id   it*

as if   this smidgen   this *tittle*   were manna   it is
there is   some crucial next-to-nothing   it stands for

of & by   & with   & in   us too

~

Glare-iotas they flee up bored thrills into chalk-dust

motes   those girls   I sat behind in class   & braided their hair
instead of working   sums / dates   who later put out   & were torn open

in front   by men   for children   they gave me their hair   to play with

then did not know me   at recess   but I half-remember   names
faces   & here I replicate   our little secret   the calm gift   a trust

bestowed me   this dork behind them   sits at the same   shame-words

& works in threes to make   sacred repair   out of each bunched   strand
as rise   *flit*   tiny wisp-hairs   lost to any pattern   *lit*   havering

from *harja* (army)   & *waldaz* (rule)   comes praise   *to herald*

almost only light   those women   in Ontario still   or far   or dead
& me   also   then as now   little else than light   holding light

~

J O Y

a hook   *&* a dowsing stick   either side   of a well
the hook   depth & hunger

the dowsing stick   affinity & intuition

depth & hunger   affinity & intuition
the well   open to these

~

You cannot write a poem about a fly
without knowing *The Fly* by Holub

nor a poem about an eel

without knowing *The Eel* by Montale
nor a poem about a fox

without remembering *the hot stink*

of Hughes's *Thought-Fox...*
but there are centuries of horse poems

& still the horse is not *The Horse*

it is wiser to devote oneself to *drawing* horses
with brushes made of horse hair

in each stroke the tail seeks the fly

~

Reading   bored   out of my tree
I look up   the word   *word*

there it is   the root   of my problem

bored into its tree   ignoring its definition
pointing at itself

~

My posture   crumbling   says its word

quick-ache-to-sternum-slump
  but the little sweet Tommy Sweets

grown off of one last tree   beside the furthest stile

up Devitt's Settlement   *scrub cedar   mullein   purple thistle*
are down   all down   derry-down

warty-yellow in the unscythed timothy

my posture says   *I never went there   when I could*
& can't now   but I did   always did   & am

~

I work on a poem   nearly a year

when it is aping nothing else   & everything else
  when its music is quirky-intrinsic   its tone a   *ping*

when its shapes on the page   are a delicate Calder mobile

 of balance   quivering   poised in the air
the arrogance of all this astounds me

~

For a few pages   each day
I seem to have lurked upon   how to assemble

all that still haunts   or nags   into

separate from myself
one *hold*   that doesn't quite   *hove*

but feels as if   it might   any mo/ now

for some next   nether-attender
what more defy / admit

to ripple-chord   this poised else...

~

On my study door   *The*

cut as a stencil   through white tin
in my study window   another stencil   *seconds*

The   seconds   my pc password   *theseconds*

crank each lock open   to green-grey
undertow-blooms   down the Trent-Severn

my study   that's a laugh

I don't study   *I doubt myself*   in here
garrisoned by   all these rangy   props

~

Remember   the word   nothing

when it had no   *was not*   language
stripped of its capital N (1914)   unitalicized yet (1968)

give it   should   let it   must   you argued

(remember   the ember   in remember
you spat on it   as too melodic)

~

Bygone's unboiled awe   ear-etched
refuses   to let me   *not*   discombobulate

cruises   as bruises   *moment*   as *nonent*

goddamn Uncle Rat   chicanery & malfeasance
hear my little stink-songs   or don't

against hearsed usage!

~

As Colin Browne says
what awaits us   each morning

is this spoon   the sentence

I put the handle   in my mouth
set an egg   in the oval   & run

but how to   ferhoodle it   unhandle it   & find

a *Wilson's Bowl*
like Phyllis did   a coracle   serving

invited   & offered   up

wait wit   no game   as in a race
no system-click

as in claim

~

Although moss   covers stone

though it takes on   stone's shape
it does not want   to be stone

it does not want   the stone to stop   stoning

it does not want
moss works away   at its processes   to go on

without metaphor   or story   so I tell you   forget

> *to the stone's turned back*
> *moss whispers nothings*

> *& slowly the stone cracks*

instead   embrace   only pattern
furthering   only pattern   ruined

as nearly-not   in air-ity   if-here-ness

~

While tanks grunt   *valour*   on Parliament Hill

I try to recall   was it last winter   or the winter before last
John attended to   the needs of that   little tree frog

fed it flies & crickets   even took it in a basket   on a road-trip with him

 this week it seems   like an act of protest   how Marie knows
what we always order   for breakfast at Peter's   I keep sneaking down

to where a river was   as if *worth*   were moral   25

~

Dryness   warmth   toys

sit   & be an animal   in a room
with   & of   the light in it   *spoking*

you   kept in it   your shape   your sell-outs

 cages of shape
 a zoo of cages   a zoo of all shapes

 stop writing   this pap

be out of it   feed   the other animals
 your point   to dull it

draw

~

Kinds of poetry:

1

2 I miss it...

3 *I've had it!*

4 Lampoon. Inherit. Bestow.

5 It: big hitching-post / little church

6 *eye tea*

7

(1 & 7 are not the same)

~

Done   I run down to the like   *the lake*
with pruning-shears

to cut the mobile up   throw each word on the water

then stand & watch   my complicated   indecisions
slop about   *willy-nilly*

the earth's   unexponible crevices   own my songs now

go forth wee boke
by rogue-*errance*   not arrogance   confound

~

3-toed   Mother   of us all
humping it   through craw-mud   stone now

an M-dash   the fossil   of her baton

/

Each entry   concentric   to shore
these disturbed ponds   my open knuckles   I drag

a bogus hunger-legend   up onto   another page

⊙

Stem   system   toll   systole
the word-plow passes   then comes back   airborne

where it held the line   now it swoops   a flourish

//

Two slits   scratched close   on smoked glass
I read   our past century's shame   through Stein   & Weil

their tracks   make the manned borders   fibrillate

/

Terrible the word-plow   nosing sense along   but worse
worse   the ploughshare returning   as a scythe-blade

to sign   as if conducting   its quick jot through us

~

I am in two anthologies

the one everyone is in
 & the one no one is in

~

If you come by   & I'm not home
I'm at your place   in my clown pants   & Doc Martens

a lighthouse's shadow   its bobby-pin's grip   on the sea

~

A pen makes a great cork

from an early sonnet of mine
 only this one epigraph survives

but at the antique market in Perth

 I bought these cast iron chisels
a complete alphabet of punches

 & a complete set of number-punches

they sit in two wooden blocks
 with holes for each punch to stand upright

maybe I won't have to pander to silence

 or rely on persnickety templates
but can be more like Greg Curnoe

 inking by hour those big stamp-letters

he put his whole body into
 spelling   *trivial*   g - l - o - r - y

what still holds my tongue down?

~

That slight crunch when I turn my neck
to look out the study window   *hey*   wild turkeys in the yard &

the *hot stink*   of Meat Boy   his enduring nearness

he doesn't say anything anymore   the drink was his larynx
I can get all full of myself   lost tinkering   & forget he's still there   here

chewed skinless by a secret   inconsolably 8

he is afraid the stupid turkeys will shove their heads in his mouth
I forgive no one

~

The gleaming   empty bed
of the gravel truck   I am lost in

told to stay   *the hell outside   for an hour*

dented   load upon load   enticed
by the noise   of rock dumped   the violence

& cursing   of my father's week away   *come home*

at my sister's wedding   Cec would put a matchbox   filled with rusty nails
in the glove compartment   of the flaming black   honeymoon coupe

Bob   chew one each night   to keep your strength up

a geomancy   the details   unto families   pretend
say grace   buy us _____   *chant bitter   cling long*

I am on all fours   my last ditch   to act the smart dog   Lassie

in that slightly tilted   hoist-bucket
7   already fucked   yowling

~

Again   drive south   between   the dull fields

worse off   to have visited   /   better now   to aim away
under me   asphalt   *the ass   the fault   & my initials*

Highway 35's   far tip   a silver-black   sheen

when I do   get that far   there will be   no shine
just mulch   scarred by frost   & bloody quills

I keep   telling myself   how distance   is health

but escape is a joke
my escape-songs   are a joke

~

Rabbits   & voles   *girdle*   my lilacs
deer   eat the new   purple-red   buds

so   I spray   the branches   with *Bobbex*   (coyote urine)

to defend   bouquets   like any   old   nature poet
no   a better poem   than I was writing   has come   to kill me

& I am   trying   to tell it   to piss off

*Complexity   overdetermines   Subject
toward   Impurity-Design*

~

Dead robin   full of worms

dead worms   full of earth
 the sycamore   in dusk light

balancing   its vow   *permanence*

 dead words   full of dead ears
my sin is that I love

 the word *amphora*   more than the amphora

it would point to   if I let it
 mystery   does not exist   in meaning

but in the lyric filter   self   as usage flows

 sound   be texture   *am ph   or a...?*
each tree shadow   verbless   clocking

 is Marco Polo   to its blind root

each word   the modern China   of its etymology?
Ss on flagstones   *sight & seer*

living earth   living robin

~

 Few poems worth knowing

worth suspect   *knowing* suspect   *few* suspect
 seeing double   hearing less out of one ear

to have had to be 60 to say in a poem the abuser's name

 is success   or failure   *both / neither*
my tongue's baloney-smell   articulating   *adios*

~

The line between   your silence & mine
that could not be crossed anymore

bent   by distance & time

into bundles of letters   in drawers
 each letter   in each word

twisted   into its shape

from that old line   that nearly smothered us
by its straightness

how silence hides   in O's mouthiness

in S's cul-de-sacs
 in the dunce-cap A swallowed Δ

in Y's hod

~

If I walk to the dock

with my coffee   at dawn
 & sit on a log

in the fog   near the loons

 don't tell Gertrude
on me

~

Gap   hum   gap
any small word   for instance   *has*

(*h*: the sibilant entry   *a*: the luthier-fruit   *s*: the susurrant outrush)

has   no noun slathering at its arabesques
  no verb tagging along   hungry for the straight-goods

State goods   the statement-gods

  a possessive   *has*   owns only itself   lines   near-circles
  a syllable   a digit-citizen

  by number   *has*   is a palindrome   8 1 18   which means nothing

or what about that other tiny possessive   *my*
  now *my*   is more of an   *in vitro* strum   than a *gimme*

& if written as numbers

  my would be   13 25   which means nothing
  it is as if   by denying

  these little words   their tug   at meaning

I could   *unwith*   myself
 & so   *colloidal*   become   only quick notes   that defy

any obligation   a word might have   to point

  at this livery   ground
gap   hum   gap

~

Awoke at 6   trode   lid-mania   started fir ( )   wiss

I'm out   to exacerbate   the smug word   *did*
  before it grows   its tumorous *e*   *died*

umbrage   humbrage   ~~humbrag~~   humage!

~

I can heft & aim a logging-hammer's blacksmithied X

unused for a hundred years can swing it home into rings of pulp
as accurately & as legibly as it did in 1900 at the Boyd camp

this martial puffery of repetition keying enjamb laser

I would keep at a hard-mark level *one line crossing one line*
where many lines crossing many lines conceive a darkening

an illiterate-eclectic net for light high up a smudge-knot our nest

~

My left side won't wake up

inextricable in its abandoner's congregation
a blur a slur *oblivitu* an endless *not-quite* a give

a lallia-rangle undergoing

/

My right side can't sleep

it is pinned at invention auditions scrutiny
detailed to this scared parsed one-off

novelty a new kind of loneliness

~

A charmed life   well I   never thought I'd write   down

such a slap-worthy   brag   but today Phyllis Webb   called me
from Ganges   February 28th   *I'm in bloom*   Victoria!

Ontario a far slog   the only coat I need now   my old jean jacket

the shadow of AC/DC   still recognizable   on the back
all that metal   *fetal*   grind   beckons a choice   not to wallow

to be *charmed*   bp might say   is to *c*   *harm*   35

I do   chart who & when   do cup fear-sites still   but the stain
has to be patched   daily   the numb scar   is not luck

I *court*   my blessings   by distance & proximity   by pen

~

Voice   you still have a harness on

but consider   evince   the word   *harness*
how italicizing it   slips its harness   half-off

draws attention to it   as a word

puts its use   out to pasture
pull nothing   but yourself   old word

now shoot the horse-metaphor

be only yourself   old word
hey stop addressing it   as if it were sentient

har / ness   good   say again   *har / ness*

two syllables   both stressed   / /
now   at long last   might you   Voice

ponder   *harn*

~

Doing great

is a warm baguette   & olive oil   in France
  hoity   but no mouth

doing not-so-great

  is margarine   marge   a hoyden
all mouth   but no bread

not even Wonder Bread   up Bury's Green

  pinch & smear   any cheap   dye-pouch
  margin   call it   grateful

& dig that pen in

~

  I send you silence

  the kindness of no metaphors
   or stories or platitudes or news

  too often while saying

   what might be said
  I have missed how an empty page

   is a sacred space between

  two words that are the same
   like us

~

Breathing out slowly
they will tell you   I have gone

training   a kind of fear

looking right at me   they will say
he is no longer with us

training   a chorus of fear

in the same extravagant breath
they will assure you

I am at your side

an ancient chorus
infear / outfear

don't be ridiculous

~

Then   one word   after another
will let me in   without breath   or   if

a word   I don't know   unpronounceable

which one   a verb   a vowel   an armada shelf's
septum-glare-curl   impatient   kind   as

the letter O   shall finally deign   or   to let me in

& then   my larynx-fossil   a violin-kayak
the clanging chevrons   the full Waterway   is

will open   each lock   each prow drop   stripped

of its number   its rank   one word   any
after another   without breath   at lake's end

this last   it   forgetful-vast   a   vow-try

~

I am still ashamed   & in awe   of what compelled me
to arrange   greasily   at 5   a first little shelf   of titles

between me   & my family   the fortress wall   my *no*   I

have always vanished   read   lilted   many books   in hand
to compost   a voice swiped / blown   whereas   by library

might form   an enervation   dare I type *waft*   or scratch *petal*

but the stare & sleep   of no books   the as if   blank Speller
my father   the hunter   attracts me   more & more   his

I thought   stupid   *silent footing*   grows   a comfort

I like to get up   before my books   these fire-break   days
& go out into the fields   with my nettle tea   where listen

beyond the Pale   hesitancies   un-at   red   wilting   akin to

voices   as near as I can tell   a complexity-willingness   is
trying to let my *no*   soften   to a *naw*   & then   give up   as

a long *ah*   at last   among other deliquescent   near-circles

breaking surface   the lack of sound   I strain within   or am
has a shaggy   soggy   tongue   *waft-petal*   it smells   most

final   more & more   I'll be   all for that

~

Phere   *situ inboca*

II · The Chase

Festivities

Oh I missed Fountain Pen Day!

~

For a while   a couple years ago
I was working on a series of poems about imaginary Special Days

somewhat in imitation of Calvino's *Invisible Cities*

my favourite was *Day Day*
 all of the festivities for this one   were transparencies

they fit   right over the day   & were unseen

~

Also   this line   *no one remembered it was Balcony Day*
seems so sad   that line   to me   even now

~

Once a year   there was a day   *by which*

anything you wanted to keep   had to be taken off your balcony
then   on that day   Balcony Day

whatever items   were still left out there   *disappeared*

all of the balconies   up all of the high-rises   in all of the target areas
suddenly empty

what a feeling of lightness   & a readiness   for fresh marketing

Cashier Co-operatives would send up flares from their roof-decks
as if ice has broken in a river   enthused the laureates

sales soared

~

But   if a person were standing on a balcony
at midnight   come Balcony Day

poof   gone

so   *balcony*   as in   *she committed balcony*   or   *he balconied*
became a common form of suicide   annual group suicide

~

It was good to clear away the dead-profit junk every 12 months
but how could the State stop these suicides by its consumers?

so   all advertising for Balcony Day   was suppressed

& each year   *Clearing Day*
as it was now called   in internal reports

was scheduled for a different   undisclosed   day

~

That helped   but still there were many who   sick of shopping
stood on balconies every night   at the tick of midnight

hoping today   was the day

Vancouver 1980

That spring Fred ate only cherries
then all summer it was carrots   he bought an industrial juicer

& his skin turned yellow

he went to his Food Co-op's solstice party nude
 as a squash personified

~

After Rothenberg & the Four Horsemen at the Western Front

Barry said   *come along to Warren Tallman's party*
Goodchild snuck into Linda's new place after midnight

& into her rented room   luckily she wasn't there

he took his *Raven* manuscript back   then he arranged her gladiolas
& all of her shoes   into a mandala on the floor

~

If I was out of my gourd   on cheap Chinese cooking wine
at Spanish Banks   at 4:30 AM

the Vietnamese fishermen   would be lowering their hinged grills

baited with chicken-scraps
 into the harbour's   sawdust & oil   slop-lights

~

The hottest women worked at Rape Relief

but you had to join the Men Against Rape collective
& take Radical Therapy workshops

& do fundraising for the women's shelter

you had to *get it*   you were a potential rapist   *I got it*
bill bissett gave me a stick of Astro gum

44   I still have the wrapper

~

Gordon ate what Fred ate   was tonsuring early

& played the flute   eventually he took a woman-friend too
& taught her to care as deeply as he did

about the angle the carrots were cut at

~

Later they'd haul their traps back up
& when they saw the crabs   where the chicken-parts had been

they'd start talking   for the first time all night

Vietnamese   really fast   *to me*
this snippy tintinnabulation

~

34 years later   if I get up early enough
afraid of nothing   & afraid of everything   are no different

a sec   distance

only bric-a-brac   in a white space
that is mine to fill

Tremolando

Two women squat in the woods   peeing   the young one says
these flowers tickle   tender as the first touch   should have been

the old one snorts & says   *grow up Honey   our eggs is Troy upon Troy*

& all them big dicks is just shadows   trillium shadows
random in a breeze   enlivening   our fabled   leaf-mulch

~

Danté Gabriel Rossetti   that's the name I was looking for
& what a name it is   his Arthurian ornations

or John William Waterhouse's   *Windflowers*

both come to mind   when I look at these art class photos
your dad took of you   *pretty fair maiden*

I am thrilled by   in proud-husband ways   & in lecher ways

a brave young soldier riding by
she got here pretty safely   as yourself   to old me

~

Wow   but the final time

we share love   draws nearer
then there will be   almost nothing   adamant

left to relinquish   you & I

will begin   to take separate trails
that wend   close enough together   for holding hands

at last   the indifferent body   will be free   if cruder

we will taste it   get down   off its cow
hear it   begin to swear   by love's   opposite

to never have to go home again   ever

~

When you don't know the egg is hard-boiled
& give it a spill-tap

or when you think you are on the bottom step / but there's one more

the look   vast   you get then
we haven't known each other long enough

not nearly

~

Marriage   threefold threshold   rising scale
carrot   road repair   oriole

The Chase

Bobcaygeon   1968   the Ohioans
camped   all summer   above Kimble's Dam

had piped-in water   change rooms   a loading-dock

we had an outhouse   a half-pump in the pantry
plastic curtains   calcium side-roads

their sons' parts   zippered in paddies

their daughters   swung kinked   Joplin-tresses
their little   boyish   leathery wives

butting-out   angrily   to calculate the exchange

on a 25¢ packet of sinkers   in The Buckeye
kisses   tips   they geared   their swaying

Winnebagos   off our beach   Labour Day weekend

water-lap   a torn-page vacancy   up still-smouldering sites
there's a stink   in the rust maples   muskie heads

& pickerel heads   even this late   & jigged carp heads

each mouth   gagged wide   with a popsicle stick
then spiked   on a branch   as a trophy

~

To orchestrate   the unextravagant
leaf thru   set-phrases   yr index   lights on

course I can   might as well be

the celluloid vine   under tongue   drying
all verbs bereft   *to be*   especially

snooty couplet   languorous epithalamion

aloft   in the knobbed orchard   yr butterfat chest
unassuaged   usual   cut-rate

no one   now owns   wow

~

To not let poetry be furniture

milled from an *arbre de la liberté*
 how every word chosen sets out to save us

from shame & earn us praise

past that   the chase   of an odd lilt   in the vowels
past that   Time dies   & Colour   & all frames

we usher noises   Legend owns   & inlays

the boy who gunned down the crossing guard
 for his school video project   grade 5

in the bath I saw the tick had burrowed its welt at my groin

pinched it out   called Telehealth   a nurse named Monique
I dreamt Bök was showing the cops where the little chansons

were buried   in toppled fridges   *risk cubed*

I propped the hammered muddy basil up
  on kindling-sticks   & wrote

the Old Testament sky   in all its loud Spring Lines

is still one piss-poor substitute   for a leaf
we will cower   along a bulldozed ridge

& be hunted by   the un-read-to

~

A train is passing   one boxcar usurped   by a fat tag   RELISH   49

there's a company in China   could make a Greek column for us
  they will cut   *a mountainside of marble*   load it   onto an open barge

& chart course for Venice   a crew of chisellers on board   *as the container*

crosses the ocean   the crew   carves the column   hear the c-words
siren   & attack   the white I   its waste marble   edited   into seas

all that chiselling   *& depth*   all that tapered   heavy   *eloquence*

Corinthian / Ionic / Doric   *the sweep*   a saga / trilogy   *the expense*
  plus metaphor   Black Swallowtail   early-hatcher   ripe in its phase

voracious   light   on hand   its prober screwing   this honey-swab   lure

OK Golden Age   OK sucky flutter   OK verb-trespass   OK silence   yep
idling   at dawn   by every trestle   as barrier-lights flash   bored stiff

we don't all want to   go back to school   or eat while flying   or read

~

I will quote Yeats   anyway   *tough*   who   when
grey & giving up   instead of fame   & its cape   wanted

to be *colder*   *& dumber*   *& deafer*   *than a fish*   I still say

defiance   to young poets   in workshops   *patience*   you need
to find   like Yeats   your   *sword upstairs*   & bury it

down by the riverside   I am rated   for the fables   as-if-of-self

I recite   handle-first   the woman who couldn't attend
had to welcome home   the troops   she was the Laureate

for the Highway of Courage   *I'm not kidding*   *f$%+.x*

still   near ersatz Innisfree   Bishop's old fish   story   leaps
selfish   ruthless   private   & silent   fending song

its arc   the lyric slash   sated   on midges

~

Scrapes   are my yields   as I honk by
the prize-winning   4-H stalls   of Fair Day

adios to barns   *in lofts / attacks*   *& sprees*

with giant rhubarb   my dray   laden / posted
from Kinmount   to Coby   thrown butts   burn arcs

is my team drinking   *in summertime*   *near Fenelon*

I clowned along   guzzled   rutted & wed   awhile
leave yr home   in the rear-view / you   bushwhacker

who will Cezanne   *our frost-patched*   *horn-sumac now*

my whole *etc*   the humming   canal lights   on
this collector-ramp   a tar smear   sans serif   uncial

red nose   *come off*   *allow serene*

Poor

Scared   words   jump
over   fly up   scat sing   Ovid

doe → *dove*

~

Arrowheads   Δ   keepsaken   Δ   in displays
& the sieges   bronzed   fog...

livestock   Δ   accounted for   Δ   in cuneiform...

book-learning   starts   at the fulcrum
but this fenced pasture   or landscaped park   or square

is that same   adjective-sundering   battleground

under the word   *reason*
you can still make out the word   *hunger*

if you know how to read

(or maybe   if you *don't*   know how to read
the palimpsest   is starker)

~

Brandish   *a cappella*   these latticed   guilts
crack   ordinance   &   ordination

~

In that township   of inherited farms

we were barn swallows   *alighting momentarily*
on a busted step-chair   on its side   in the road

no we weren't

~

Spell   *converted sheep pen for rent*
a photo   of the young Queen   holding Charles

a baby picture   stuck to a wall   over a bullet hole

no   we weren't
deserving   of any   similitude

~

What the labels   on the cans   shouted   was in them
Fruit Cocktail   Creamed Corn   Pork & Beans

SpaghettiOs   Water Chestnuts?   boldfaced   dented   lies

each donation   had been church-filled   with rust
eventually   the shot   flattened   cans

in the woods   kicked   admitted it

~

Take it all   these

inconsequent   unwashed   *slights*
yr   pre-Christ   shame   &

translate them   *it*   into   *sleights-of-hand:*

above a fence   *a doe*
its hoof's aim   a beak   *v*

dove!

~

As a No One   hunt   a Many

gather   *aim*   gather-aim
nouns   by chipping   *past*   a point

in mud   in wax   /   of mud   of wax

count   *whose?*   beeves
draw   embroider   *embellish*   mesh

arrowheads Δ cow heads Δ cap A

& the rooftops Δ *war housing*
see   say   *skrawk*   tell

how Class is denied   by enforced separateness

blather   without Art
which is Character's city name

(says Kavanagh)

~

Collaborate   paper   black
write   *aggregate*   *flock*   *mortar*

keep a tally   *roof's pitch* Δ *insul*   *insultar*

answer   *cheap*   to guess   *safe*   *& dry*
take home   yr F   insult   as habitat

tell on   *imitation brick*   (its bite-smell)

~

One long tillage

between   the Buick's wheels
one crop   weeds   caught   in the chassis

crawl under   hack at them   harvest them

use this stick   gooped with oil
wipe it off   on the side-grass   like hatred

54   not really   *yes really*

~

Do not   act out   or attend   Shame Theatre
don't you dare shut up

whisper   *I am here*   X

~

Ordination   &   ordinance   mock

flourish   by   & in   these latticed   guilds
these tiny   Δ   *splitting-wedges*   Δ   *sung*

no way it's over

The Opened Locks

Unsound   many   & offering   merely
attention   *the natural prayer   of the soul*

says Malebranche   I am terrified   of my skin

this largest organ   this catastrophe's edge   *growing*
touch   its dialect   I write in   & sleep in

this dismantled   bed / flower   betrayed corpus

rashes   open sores   melanin   lip-service
BEWARE BULL   it says on the fence   in that photo

of Basil Bunting   *overfalls sketch a ledge*   laughing

why not   turn the crank   to open   the swing bridge
open the locks   allow   the rapids   *rapidity*

it's crazy   & dangerous   white / rocks   but a blatant

madrigal   still only May   & my Christmas notebook
spine-broken   undecipherable   nearly used up

I cower in it   & leap   scratching   semblance   raw

where the second o   becomes an r   in *wood*
to become *word*   in the woods   on wood

I hear   a drop   o   branch & growl   r

into   circles & folios   ripples & portmanteaus
butcheries & veils   Niagaras   of old   war letters

who was it   defined a letter   as a pot   to PS in?

my skin   is my Batoche   my ambassador
my pampas   in this shameful   ass-is-grass   current

my larynx   is a singing frog   *ph/legm*

it wens & barks   stems & hides   blinds & meres
attending   at the lip   of silence   an offering

I fall / am a falls   one   glare-sheet   sound

III · Artery

One water this   language this   other blood

all of us   underground   thrown together   shadows   blanks
as interconnecting lines   rush us   sitting-standing

see the grease-spots   our sleep has worn   vassalage through steel

my hand is asleep   an inflated glove   full of wet sand
but liquored up   can we ever shake   *mama the staggers & jags*

let's drink   affinity   from any test-tube   no heirs

no sire-spatter   here's to   shared   anonymity
I drifted off   plot-numb   mulch   half-here   a useless bastard

from no noble line   *Family Tree Drops Branch on Sex in Tent*

& at evening   came to rest   beneath a loud oak   magnolia   lime
lit by all manner   of bird-gods   who   as I slept   convened

a hybrid congress   beak-snaps   *polly-wants*   déclassé

I dream *rivulet*   get *offal*   my burrowed colours   do not pass
but in wild repose   hurtling   I was set upon   by a brush   a quill

& did transcribe   into a chained scribbler   the menagerie

of those proceedings   *The Rantos*   complaints   yells   reports
tapestries   epistles   by those   of those   on behalf of those

for whom   *blood means nothing*   except oppression

therein   whereby   the lyric   splayed open   & glowed
a lesson fossil   a mute knot   no more

~

A Pope   his robes immaculate   underwrites blood
Luke 3:23–38   my eye asleep   gibbous leaking

blind to how it hails   my foot asleep   elusive   Big Foot

the President throws a bag of blood   a crowd claps   a ball game starts
my heart   sound   asleep to philosophy   too busy fisting its tides

the Prime Minister rings the President   *what should I do with all this blood*

the President says   *freeze-dry it by sending it to committee*
unpronounceable   on the subway   *the grub-way*   early   late

we are recent immigrants   reading 100 bibles   transiting to crap-jobs

the Governor General looks up   at a Spirit painting by Norval Morrisseau
then smiles & says   *this buffalo mozzarella is superb*

the official culture thinks we are vermiculture   because we disown shame

to sit here   nodding   all of us late   translators
blod bloet Bloor bluot   bloma Place-d'Armes   sanguis haima

Premier's Breathalyzer Off Chart   Mayor Watches Vampire Movie Nude

my doctor throws down in disgust a Norman Bethune biography
I don't care how I came by these looks   or what station I got on at

language this   other blood   *Finnegans Wake* 3:23–38

Norval Morrisseau   voiceless   dry   on display at the National Gallery
in a wheelchair   among his metamorphoses   cries for us   cries us

~

BLOOD   A MYTH OF FAMILY   (*CESSOR*)
consider the nativity scene   portico   couple & child

attendant shepherds   animal figurines

FAMILY   A MYTH OF HISTORY   (*AM I MY…?*)
that manger   *that manager*   its silhouettes   its story

all year   on our church roof   as model   as caution

a lineage-obedience   virus   in every outpost
HISTORY   A MYTH OF PROGRESS   (UP   & TO THE RIGHT)   61

don't think it didn't help us   talk those redundant   glass floats

McKees & Dunvagens   into giving up   their juniper dories
PROGRESS   A MYTH OF CAPITALISM   (PENTHOUSE SPRAWL)

resilient as soaked rope   stare down the sea   they could

but were sentiment-scuppered   at the run's end
tamed   by the big star   X   by a diet   of crèche

CAPITALISM   AN *IT ALL* MYTH   (CURRENTS IN VAULTS)

we unsettled every last   bobber   from those fished-out villages
relocated yr legend   & yr tall-tale   into the nearest cities

to babysit   gaming grandkids   feed lapdogs

CURRENCY   (FT KNOX)   A MYTH OF SECURITY
in the Queen's   blued perm   Lucifer   coughing

his profile   the regimented wave   the pounded seal

SECURITY   A MYTH OF IMMORTALITY   (KEY-RING HALO)
now turbaned Magi   repel from clouds   bearing test-samples

now hooded guards   watch over our sleep

they monitor   our conjugation   under this animal roof
IMMORTALITY   A MYTH OF BLOOD   (BEGAT)

BLOOD   A MYTH OF FAMILY   (*CESSOR*)…

~

I am with the adopted

who have been ruined by a story
 we are starving for

starved by   an official story

 we have been told it
is our destiny to know

a story we could just as easily make up

 it might suit us better
 I am walking beside *insemination*

surrogate   WolfBoy   clone

 talking with unknown soldiers   navies
lost names in old photos

 an outdated heritage myth

keeps us focused on our laps
 keeps us as if lapdogs

we are hurting ourselves for evidence

 begging for legitimacy
 language this   other blood

 transformation the only iv

~

In dream   those woven lines   carding   we shook 'em

when I came to   *my arm   my hand   my eye*   it was   as if
hydro   were linking   pin by pin   each place-name

after a blackout   Iceland   Ireland   Van Diemen's Land   Poland

Easter Island   Switzerland   Baffin Island   Boyd's Island
Africville   South Porcupine   Mozambique   Kyoto   Gozo

the doors are closing   opening   I have missed my stop   63

as passed out   amanuensis   I had disowned   blood's proof
was no longer bogged at source   or log-jammed by corpus

the oak   magnolia   lime   adjourned   /   the birds   mere   birds

spiral-glinting   screwy   mumbled   loops
you & I   who & why   uneven   syllables   gulfs   deltas

one water this   language this   other blood

but then   when the wars   over blood   were no more
the wars   over water   began

IV · The Rogue Wave

As they colonize   they peep   a roar

I am a mess   so how does the poem   accrue…
I dreamt   I could type   sense   at random

without rhetoric   or divination   to waft like merging flocks

4i, ehs ofh woa zm woehf 40 a.f jwofjl rihld rhlfd'p
ei thsm lx' Jof ri rigue sr o ri gro erfj

from messes like this   rough-typed   I thought I might salvage

accidental words   /   the results   were pure crap
almost no signifiers   usually just consonants   scraping

a perplexity   unpronounceable   no music   no Joycian puns

what an idiot I was   to invite   by winging it   *Sir Sense*
on guard   behind his   squealing   arrowslits

~

First Thought   as in   *First Nation*   designates
not only   or always   chronology   but   *primacy*

beneath First Thought   a compromised mulch   of jingles

& platitunes   then   farther down   gladiators' names
unspaced   hammered into bronze   woe's woo   9 layers under

& below all that   jam-packed   cold   fiddle-faddle   a grunt

there weren't enough   intervals   between the letters   I typed
my hands only knew   2 or 3 shapes   to pound out

vne.xkffgps,xhf   tnthmdhv,gjg   try it   if you don't believe me

all-over-the-map   *send word*   we say   /   then the deluge
lexicons   hat pins   Goyas   audiograms   tarred wrens…

goop   followed by   the televised clean up

~

Wordsworth's list   *rocks & stones & trees*
is a giving-over   of redundancy

to established rhythm   a versifier does this

a poet   hobbles our traces   to the variables
even a Snyder title   *August on Sourdough*

is composed of   2 u's   & 2 u's   t-tottering on

that little *on* in the middle   a balance   worked-across
by a 5-syllable   jazz pattern   *ah uh ah ow oh*

with 2 sounds matching   *ah ah*   for repetition inside variation

Wordsworth's words   called *done*   are carapaces
in the glare-flux   *rocks & stones*   *impecunious*   *etc*

only a contrapuntal rhythm   a caution-tartan-grid   straining wider

can keep us   magnified-participatory   here
even the word *gravitas*   has been compromised

it once belonged to Neruda   now it belongs to The Dixie Chicks

there are too many Wordsworths
which is why Zukofsky

by *notarikon*   find *temenos*

~

At   is   circular arrows   un-aiming   *at   is*

if I say   I have escaped from   *the prison*   of metaphor
you will know I haven't   listened   long enough   to the loons

calling *loon*   in Loon   an urge to go   but wherefore

unfinished   *what-the*   ear-scribble   *ounds* (Scots)   + hunger
now does the poem   find its rogue wave   & then why shore...

~

O how we fed   on those fly-by-nights   the journals
their earthy swells *Alphabet   Waves   Gripsack*

Rune   The Ant's Forefoot   Echo   Ellipse

*Germination   Field   Impulse   Eclipse   Sun Dog
Gronk* TISH   *Swift Current   3¢ Pulp*

the ROM specimen-drawers   of those bleeding   mimeos

the music-stand   shoals   of those art-sectioned   quarterlies
what seasonal laurels bestowed   what kiss-ass imitations

& little silver mouth-offs   *aleap*   all afternoon to

sit in the numbness   of the Reference Library   & eat *lang*
to long to be caught   a herring   *a hearing*   among

~

The word   *any*
unspells itself   blearing   down the shingle

I am no gardener   or revolutionary

what does it matter   mean   but sound   which words go where?
the shore swore worse than the horse...

our epithets were sanded smooth by a coward in a high-hat...

not a living soul was reading Browning that glorious afternoon...
it takes a million wings to make one wing

~

Inside *murmur*   spectres   armies   mobs
a thousand young men from Paris a day   dying in the trenches

1916   many of the British dead   Hugh Kenner tells us

had copies of Pound's *Cathay*   under their muddy tunic-flaps
if you are coming down through the narrows of the river Kiang

please let me know beforehand   & I will come out to meet you

Gaudier-Brzeska   from the trenches   just before he died   wrote
I shall present my emotions by the arrangement of surfaces

~

A frenzy   an itch   jigs   bats   slugs   by us

faith-making   crazy to go   a potato-wind
all the poets were killing themselves for the weekend

Blanchot's *disaster*   =   responsibility for the inexpressible

absences   can't draft patterns   or can they?
so let's make a bad little toy out of the tsunami

the rogue wave   =   filthy lucre

that's the cheapest kind of anthropomorphism
applied to   a destructive force   *metaphor at its worse*

give the wave an eye-patch   a hoop-earring

it doesn't fit our calibrations   we can't predict
what it will do   *it is not our responsibility*

subtext   Random   is bad

~

Jimenez   *bad is closer to good than is mediocre*

Notley   *no pronoun shakes like body*
watch *once*   the number   become *once*   the past

take a moment   to love the word   *ample*

 try not to *pay*   attention   /   *lend*   an ear
Earth is getting an extra second on Saturday

V · Essay on Legend

They   *poisined*   his blind hound   Moses   1915

someone   a neighbour   *& how the misspelling*   *tightens it*
stiff detachable collar   ribbon tie   vest & hunting jacket

double-barrel shotgun ready   Lloyd George mustache

the snow bloody by the back stoop that morning
locked in   chased out   a him a her an it   panicking

on newspapers   in the mud-room   *Ypres*

see these deep gouges in my pine door   both sides
claw-sheaths rucking lake ice   a high kicked-rib whine

this same stray dog I shoot   then Dad shoots

~

No one knows where   call him *Otty*   came from   or nearly from

a town two or three hours away   some argue   but why argue
his log cabin was shadowed   by tall white pines

on a rise above the weedy lake   from which he took his name

he loved wine   but he loved it too much   & had to give it up   for tea
no good with his hands   he came down to the writing of poems

came way down   lowly   to the writing of poems   of poems

in his later summers he cut no grass   a sea of weeds to the porch door
unless reading is grass-cutting   his word-feeder   bird-feeder

was also a log cabin   hanging from a roof-corner   of his log cabin

meta   birds came & went   *pshaw*   *festoon*   too cute a word
to cut a word   he would chastise himself   for cutesiness

~

Most days Al Purdy

wrote poems as good as Alden Nowlan
but maybe 30 times Al wrote a poem we now call   a Purdy poem

as if some days his name were All   not Al

Nowlan also   at times   sawdust flying   achieved a wider name
All-Done-Now Land   or Old In No Land

they both wrote a lot of friendly crap that sounds the same

if read now   but who can stand to read them exhaustively now
they were drinkers   & that will get a soul above itself some

as the booze digs under eloquence like surf

but Purdy seems to have   seen & heard   his over-self
he caricatured Al as All   or was that us

while Nowlan just kept writing down memories & impressions

without distinguishing small-town small-talk from the bull moose secret life
so we tend to forget him

~

How many times have I told the story

my father throwing the cat in the air   & shooting it
I have told the story   for its shock value   tons

but in truth I don't remember seeing the cat blown to pieces

I don't think I ever actually saw my father heave the cat up
& wait for it to peak   its pitch   that point at which it stops rising

there was a jet going over   a jet-trail

apogee   & just before it begins to fall   no   I did see
I was there   my sister & mother were there too

it was my sister's cat

~

He only took his glasses off   scratched & smudged   for sex   sleep

ablutions   he was *afeared* of   & cursed up & down at   the bumptious cities
he sported corny string-ties   a birch fire   dashes   banjo-tunes   fedoras

in a *withdrawn* book he fingered the cathedral windows of St Patrick's Dublin

purples & reds aimed skyward   his hates were likewise from sacred rooms
the government   smokers   enjambment   pets   meat eating   TV

golf   opera   *arggh   what was I complaining about just now   escapes me*

wherewithalling   his poems tell no daily rushes   they make rare sense-lick
as if an earlier language were rowing in him   *rhabdomancy*   lines burl

snigger   contradict themselves   imitate peepers   coy-wolves   his puns

risk a bitter laugh at our disability to read & write wide   yet are of   *of
a begrudgingly welcoming nature*   it is said   oh   &   he loved women

~

The day Lloyd Kelly got married   remember we saw him   on the road

to town   dressed up   sitting stiff in the buggy   the seeds of final acceptance
shaking in his eyes   *I'm gonna get married today*   he told us

gonna get married today   you know what that means   the stupid grin

one year later his wife decided to kill it or keep it warm   who knows why
she cooked it in the oven in their tar-paper shack up Galway Creek

but *he* took the blame   & got off   he told the judge   *the bones

of a baby cannot be distinguished from the bones of a dog*   the judge
said he was right   & let him go home   to his mother   Toots

his wife   Lil   hung out for years in the town dump   you'd see her there

~

To become a place   as local theatre   to take its name   *Otty*

to cultivate an armchair-lumberjack's voice   to sing of disasters
in the north woods   mining strikes in Michigan   Nottinghamshire 1885

to request one's ashes be taken to Greece   as an affectation

OK dump my ashes where I stand   right here   pine shadows darkening
the weedy shallows   OK I'll grin & admit it   *I merely like to pretend all this*

listen to the old bastard   wax & beg   sham-honest   rage to rags

below these cabins   the word *Otty*   glints back into its   wakesake
wherever no buildings are being built   the sounds in his poems continue

creatures   short-lived   *these creature-noises*   he quotes himself

shoot me   our mating fiddle-stones   he means *stories*   tilted   snapping
the Shield jumps   its scansion   *bucksaws   auto-harps   antennae*

O gravel-pitted highlands   O burrowed dictionary   *the   a*

~

80 Zukofskys   hyphen-dense   targetless

how to scupper the page   to a wider inclusiveness   Whitman tried
how to feminize   un-legalize   the page   Stein our pioneer

how to unleash   not by logic or precision   or metaphor

what is intrinsic   to the page
bifurcation & atrocity   syrup & the red eye

~

Anon   I   protean
try to instigate   the wolf-child sabre-line   *snick*   head rolls

minus the wolf-child   minus the sabre

not this line   but one is coming   destitute of tradition   *keening*
no encore   no embellishment   no sepia   no distance

try to stop it   Eloquence   our disease

~

Al wrote inside an A
near a town that starts with A   did he ever read Z's   "A"

who   *flow*   indefinite article   *flow*   indefinite

between   A & Z   soiled views   bull's eye dung
all *story* a metaphor-warren   the word *unleash*   the word *scupper*

epic mendacity-holes   confecturing legend

yet this constant tell-mending of the amphora
this lacing of proof   this lace roof

St Paul's dome   Ezra's forceps   a mess   so how

by warily-referential scraping   to aim
at knocked-out centres

how to   *am*   at holes

~

Taped under the full gun-rack
mom's magazine pictures   of the Queen   holding her babies

the first time I shot the 16 gauge   I was 8

kablooey   it knocked me on my arse
in Drama School   I used that same gun in a play

it cut a stark tableau   against a scrim

80   last week   a rabbit   eating my garden
I got the gun   I let it   have it

what used to explode over me   like drunken rage

is now my sole heirloom   *a pale snap*
the Queen's babies are balding

I wanted to be the Rawhide Kid

I hid inside Meat Boy instead
I wanted to be Hemingway   I am Elmer Fudd

~

Revision   is the tracks we make   when hunting doubt

he'd grab a carbon a sheet of bond sit down & type what he was thinking
it seemed as simple as that   to get very good at making it seem

a disarming   & defiant   phony   surety   we love

but pull the typed page out & write on it   then type a fresh revised page
& pull that out   & write on that one   tracking   the dubious

not second-guessing   not making First Thought more presentable

unsharpen down to the rage or joy line   the prime letting   *when she found it*
when he found it   when it found it   the poem became great   didn't it

because   to sound Blakeian a moment   the transfer of Delight abides in Wonder

which is born of Not-Knowing   what Zbigniew Herbert extols as *uncertain clarity*
or as Gertrude Stein   again   says   *it is very difficult to think twice*

in that pre-ISBN zone   pre-*reference*   between one cooked trigger

& another   waits   *reverence*   only a slight pout   Push
of lips   & tongue-tip   but vital

~

How often are we shown a poem before it is elected to represent us

regardless of merit   for instance *In Flanders Fields*
is exposure then / merit   mustard-yellow   under five dripping fox pelts

grin up at a ratchet-click & its light   *wag yr frozen tail-angel proud Moses*

~

By the spring's lip
piping from the hillside

a dipper once hung

the dipper-thief   old   drunk
 returns   parched   no dipper

he leans face-hard into the cold gush

82   the ache of the gift freely given
 eoxd kezc   soaf cdos   khitm   wlfuc

fheo   vmsl   jx hyucn   fiag

lined up behind him   waiting
 each with a cup

the whole village

~

And   to   how   with
words alone   speak   letters alone   speak

 after   the anecdotes   stop

VI · The Full Stamp

A son crawling   a job as an orderly   a white VW bug…

I was thirsty for intensity   & the cessation of intensity
 could not be thrilled enough   or calm long

~

My strutting enlistment   our gibbering shame

1 Inca   1 Hottentot   1 Polynesian   cargo
 livestock / metaphor   to England Spain France New York

curiosities   for kings queens   impresarios   85

 ceremonial   alongside eggplants us cannibals   got sick & died
very few ever made it home   rare boot-lickers adapted

cock a stove-pipe hat   cut the greasy top-knot

Calvary-heathens   honorary whistle-baggers   *bitumen-socketed*
 a poem   *a grab-sing*   has a touch-township   an I'm-zone

specific to its materials   one tribeswoman   Saarjie Baartman

 toured the Known   baring her huge ass   the Unknown
for gentry   the festivals   the citations

if any creature's song be divested of its instigation-weather…

then bruited in type   as rarified   as book-earning
 pox   to publish   is not everything

Ikinokori ikinokoritaru samusa kana
to outlive   & be oldcold   yet in awe   yet

~

At her reading   in Halifax   or Lumsden   or Comox

at Raw Sugar   or the Western Front   or the Pilot
I remembered   us two   desperate   after some launch

inverted   in a back seat   unrecognizable   *going at it*

that has got to be   20 years ago   at least   nothing of me
or her   that sang   briefly   so well   by the other's   mouth

survives   in what we sing   about   easily   these days

or in   what parts we use   to sing with   even   I sat
listening   to the blind   wet   gimme noises   we made

hurting ourselves   up into   roaring boxcars   (bad poems)

*our echo   ululation   Celtic knot   mirror   roundelay   strum
flap-doodle   constant drip...*   no one   docents   such hunger

all that posturing   as if spelling   fossilizes   into cold

thrills   that have no note   or credit   *clapping*   I came back
she would read a request   from the textbooks   "Taxi Mist"

then a new one   weird   about elk   *their wide nostrils*

while swimming   & finally   because she saw   I was there
that old villanelle   about me   I always pretend   isn't

While I careened   retsina   & Guinness w/ Irish Mist
until they were all I knew   of intensity   of rest...

~

Plié swelter   *El Diplomatico*   1939

a calligraphy-brush   we ribboned tight   to a mare's tail
a canvas we nailed   on an anchored easel   by her hocks

plagued indifference   swatting itself   flank & stifle

the blow   the caddis   the house   the tsetse   87
to draw when bitten   arcs reminiscent   of Soutine

a flute-glass rim's   wet *hum-um-um*   a Cointreau-dipped carrot

a derisive shriek   bids playing high   for the muddled oil
funds raised   to be spirited off   come Resistance

as to how all that   cut footage turned out   ask René Char

we had to eat   soon enough   with onions & brown sauce
our sensational talent   the dumb nag   *Murielle*

this fight's Masters   then as now   flies

...in Berkeley   careful Miłosz was writing   of Issa

~

We are no better off   than those punk   birches
in the hard snow   out these frosted windows

half umber   as the least of the sun   stark on the lake   lets go of us

short-lived   quick to burn   jointed like dray-horses   vacant epistolary
another snapping Jesus-January   to live right up against   double-sweatered

corralled   by rough   square logs   roofed by *Galvalume*   crowded

near birch fires   confessing   *slumped rage*   while in town   Silverados
nudge forward   at the Tim Hortons   drive-through   any hour

for that awful coffee   *a national symbol*   that tastes like   liquid cigarettes

gag me   as a Florida transport   cranks its wheels south   off Highway 7
down Gore St   I might as well   fume   a little   at the toadies   & liars

who swagger   in government   now   they have vetoed   the human

village mandate   of caring for citizens   they have outmanoeuvred
our core Samaritan impulse   *our lightning rod / pitch-pipe*   the pulse

the shared pulse   this very one   right here   *feel it*   tug   *tug*

is being rewired   emotionless   redefined   competitive   & laughed at
or press-released   as a *perky*   credit-sucking   turbine   that hates

farmland   archives   old growth   women   long-forms   discussion

stillness...   we are birches   splayed   cold black   night-locked
all our premise   appropriated   sneered at   betrayed

river by river   mountain by mountain   sea to sea

88

Kobayashi Nobuyuki
known as Issa   *One-Tea*   1763–1826

~

Lightning eviscerated our elephant jack-pine

in later storms   it opened & closed   its long wound
& moaned a moan we heard   from the dock to the cabin

until David Oliver dropped it into the swamp for us

ruined as furniture   its resin bad for the chimney
its stump   dates & events   no one had ever stood on

until I did   stuck-to   thinking of Orwell   & maelstroms   *or*

the quote was how much   to bring down our rotten white pine
onto lake ice in February   chain-saw it   split it   with the splitter

& snowmobile the wood   across the bay?   how much come spring

when the snow on the lake   erases   to notice   & commemorate
there on the ice   the full stamp   of the pine's crash   its

shadow-*thus*-ness   drawn in wet sawdust   & orange needles?

my pulpits   are Fire-Numbers   & local place-names
but I ask the Grand Concord   *what doesn't stoop to definition*

the ineffable   I hear back   *cannot be felled   by nouns*

All poets   one tea   *welcome*

~

This old wide tie   I am yanking loose   orange & green   on brown
its tongue declaims   a bright cartoon   a horse-head   a fish leaping

can't mask my rural Ontario fear   of voicelessness   or worse

of yelling myself stupid   over nothing   for attention   only to
end up   dull   dumb   of dying back into   my legacy   silence

next syllable come   get me clean away   from this Presbyterian

pinch-arsed   small town   stinking-thinking   I know   too well
may I rig   on-the-fly   inclusive junk-yard forms   that shuffle

etymology's Celtic designs   among any bewildered   outburst

stutter & burble   stomp & snort   may I braid   as cracked gift
with open-throated candour   1 my fear   2 the shore's gleaning scree

3 a *library's* silence   I don't need to flash   buffoon distractions   now

let me be still *&* bare   as I submit   to arcane collective witness
overdetermined   too far gone   *terza cadenza*   replete

VII · Amy Cosh

I am suppressing   my sexuality
August   above Otty Lake

as I listen   to crickets   & beetles

in the uncut grass   at 61   at dawn
it is as if   it is as if

~

When I try   to let
the full   shaken   sarape   rain-stick

each   tiny   bucksaw   hoist

every   grey-green   ratcheting   carapace
all the way   in   at once

I get so horny   I can't live

one second longer   like I have been
since I was 5

~

Amy Cosh was my boyhood librarian

a hump-backed spinster   she herded the grotto
of how excited   I could get   by a book

the townspeople cut her head off

full white hair   in a high bun   it is mounted
in the Municipal Offices   in Bobcaygeon

beside the head   of the bull buffalo   Old Boney

~

The women   who took sex with me
I signed for their tamped lust   they signed for mine

a scurrying harrow   a mewling vanish

I made   a moment   explode
by claiming it   as mine   by calling it   *a mine*

but now I *get*   how a moment   staggers

open   better   if shared   & unclaimed
un-played   with   or at

~

I think   somehow   Amy Cosh   *a marm*

taught me this   genderlessness   & reciprocity
years before   I was ready   to listen   to anything

but shame   & expressionism

~

Only she & I   would have been there
a late Saturday afternoon   dark November

the Bobcaygeon Library   its fireplace   is reading elm

she hands me   the crank   to the swing-bridge
she whispers   *Sunday School   is bunk*

I mean   she slips me books   by Jules Verne

or Buffalo Bill   or dull   Francis Parkinson Keyes
bad books   whose weirs glow   sedition

~

Her conspiracy   didn't preach
she pretended   to see in me   what wasn't there

quorums   I didn't have   digits for yet

she smiled   on my slapped hunger   without pity
to celebrate   the vertebrae   in the aquifer

~

She warned me
by each date-stamp   that Verulam township's

gravel pits   & potted side-roads

would fill me in   solid
with silence   or small town   piss & vinegar

if I kept sucking on   the greeting card curriculum

Home   Family   Country
one God   TV   Pets

~

Leading me   into the stacks

Amy also predicted how   the Dewey Decimal System
just might conjugate me

into heretic improvisations   perusal by perusal

pre-A   & post-Z   panoramas   scrolling
if I got away   far enough   & let it

I got away   mostly I haven't let it

~

Amy   amo   amas   amat

all of the books   I have read   or written
compose   a deep well in me

I still descend   in syntax buckets   wide-eyed

but books have also   slowly promoted   a well-cover in me
amamus   amatis   amant

my panoramas   have been floated   as rafts   to sawmills

first person   singular   *facility*
second person   plural   *folio*

third person   detentive   *Faculty   listings A to Z*

~

A locked in   locked down   sundial   well-cover
the crickets   & beetles   are chorusing   aside

like nothing   this morning   they swarm   down through

exacerbating   aroused   swamp light   in me
it is as if   it is as if

~

Maybe   I can begin   to honour   my librarian
best   if I allow myself   to be opened

& contaminated   by all these little   fuck-songs

or are these   concatenations   fuck-off songs?
high feedback surge   syllables as chiggers   wah-wah

~

Against daylight   against articulation   against precision...
not an avalanche   *not* a tsunami   *not a metaphor*

a season   of iridescent-black   feelers   in me

this busy   illiterate   noise   unveiling
its composite grunt   too big   to spell   or say

~

Amy   join me   hear me   let me
rummage   welcome   sing of   & undress   fully

this tantric   mucous   plankton   loam

twig   & cartilage   encyclopedia
I am dying into

at last   for once   right now...

Lake's End

Each morning   flaked blue   marginalia   the back porch
rotting sun   in the swamp   wet orange   bind-weed

technology   owns the air   a fine bone dust   even out here

each night   the wind   behind the news   I don't listen to
  recalibrates   the word *quality*   to force us   to use instead

quantity   (American spelling)   my job   to change it back

to heal   the folio-cuts   to conjugate   creaturely rhythms
quill   quarrel   alacrity   hilt   carbon   glint   quality

to track   compulsion's   hair-lipped   torque-promise

back down   again   into these   defiance rhythms
by way of   this lyric filter   confusion rhythms   doubt rhythms

sun   over the pines now   noted   *a loon   an osprey   jays*

early traffic   a small growing   combustion-roar   out past
the standing deadfall   in the wet grass   a scrolling line   a vole

Notes

For Ann Silversides
with Joanne Page in mind

Thanks to the Canada Council for the Arts

What I said I was going to do / got complicated & ended up as this

I have been braided / by & into the half-said

Within these invited fluxes / I found I could design past signifying

I would sing a mammal's ballad / from an undistinguished acre

"creaturely rhythms" – Wendell Berry

Thanks also to Queen's University, University of Windsor, The Banff Centre
for the Arts, & University of Ottawa, for work & residencies

Forget; Touch the Donkey; Canada Writes CBC*; * CVII*; * CMAJ*; Itty Bitty; Dusy; Poetry
Toronto; Twelfth Key; Oolichan Press; Kingston Writer's Festival; Rampike; Flat Singles
Press; boulderpavement; our hircine, murine doppelgängers, mars; Windsor Salt;
Concrete & River; The Malahat Review; The Windsor Review...*

Stan Dragland, Mark Goldstein, Erín Moure, John Steffler, Jennifer Still, Sandra Ridley...

I · Gap & Hum

madrugar – Spanish: to wake up in the earliest hours of the morning – so to make a noun
out of the Spanish verb, in this sequence (& the last one) each poem may be called a
madrugar

Early versions of some sections were published under the titles *X* (Thee Hellbox
Press, 2013) & *My Banjo & Tiny Drawings* (Flat Singles Press, 2015)

"a voice dressing up as a cricket" – Lorca

"This morning / I couldn't sleep" – after Brodsky

"I put in every part of my life. I love that. / To kiss the night, its edges, that's my kitchen." Marie Étienne. *King Of A Hundred Horsemen: Poems*. Translated by Marilyn Hacker. (New York: Farrar, Straus & Giroux, 2002)

"at the extremity of this design" – Robert Duncan

"archeological fallacy" – Peter Quartermain

Poems Worth Knowing – compiled by C E Lewis (1941); David McFadden (1971)
Past reason hated, as a swallowed bait – Shakespeare, Sonnet 129

"Novelty is a new kind of loneliness" – Wendell Berry

"*JOY*" – for Nora Gould / "I send you silence" – for Pearl Pirie

II · The Chase

Adrian Paci: *The Column* (video)

What would an innovation of the emotions feel like? What would it sound like? It would be wider than charity. It would not be composed of one voice but many. It would not be ironic.

"Pretty Fair Maiden in a Garden" – traditional song (I'll sing it for you)

W B Yeats: "All Things Can Tempt Me" / Elizabeth Bishop: "The Fish"

"glazed with rain / water" – w c w – traditional

"Vancouver 1980" – for Erín Moure / for George Stanley

"Poor" – for Jennifer Baker / "The Christmas Mummers" – Patrick Kavanagh

Nicolas Malebranche (1638–1715) / Basil Bunting: *Briggflats*

III · Artery

Began in 2013 as a response to Lawrence Hill's Massey Lectures on *Blood*

Nods to Chaucer's *Parliament of Fowls*; Alice Notley's *The Descent of Allette*; Takashi Hiraide's *For the Fighting Spirit of the Walnut* (translated by Sawako Nakayasu); & Pierre Nepveu's poem "The Woman Asleep on the Subway" (translated by Donald Winkler); Zukofsky's "Mantis" is also a subway poem

IV · The Rogue Wave

Originally commissioned by *boulderpavement*

"A slumber did my spirit seal" – Wordsworth (1798) – *"Rolled round in earth's diurnal course, / With rocks, and stones, and trees."*

"The River-Merchant's Wife: A Letter" (1915). Rihaku. Translated by Ezra Pound from the notes of Ernest Fenollosa "& the decipherings of the professors Mori & Ariga"

Robert Fones. *Anthropomorphiks* (Coach House, 1971)

"One is always nearer by not keeping still" – Thom Gunn

V · Essay on Legend

Beautiful Outlaw Press, limited edition, 2014

Biography of Master Five-Willows:

> *No one knows where he came from. His given and literary names are also a Mystery...*
>
> *At peace with idleness ... He loved to read books ... But whenever he came upon some realization, he was so pleased that he forgot to eat...*
>
> *He was a wine-lover by nature, but couldn't afford it very often ... And when he drank, it was always bottoms-up...*
>
> *But he kept writing poems to amuse himself, and they show something of who he was...*

from T'ao Ch'ien, 365–427 A D . *The Selected Poems of T'ao Ch'ien*. Translated by David Hinton. (Port Townsend: Copper Canyon Press, 1993)

"pitch" – *cf* Hugh Kenner, *A Sinking Island* (London: Barrie & Jenkins, 1987) pp 207–208

"the one   the who   cross-eyed   a falsity   that bends all sense" (Christopher Middleton: *Discourse on Legend*)

"untidy never still legend" (Richard Caddel)

VI · The Full Stamp

"Reading the Japanese Poet Issa (1762–1826)" – Cesław Miłosz, Berkeley, 1978

"My friend tree / I sawed you down / but I must attend / an older friend / the sun"
– Lorine Niedecker

"The grand concord of what / Does not stoop to definition" – Jack Spicer

"We are no better off / than those birches" – after Antonio Machado, "Today's Meditation"

VII · Amy Cosh

More *madrugar...* / for Kim Van Vliet

Library Hours: Mon & Thurs 12:30 A M–7:00 P M / Tue, Wed & Fri 10:00 A M–5:00 P M

~

...or call it all   *A Grab-Sing / A Vow-Try*

A Note on the Type

This book is typeset in both Monotype Laurentian and Slate, designed by Canadian typographer Rod McDonald. Laurentian is a text typeface family launched in 2003. Laurentian was entered in the New York Type Directors Club Annual Typographic Competition and was one of 13 designs chosen by the international jury. Slate is a humanistic sans with exceptional levels of legibility. It is a typeface of grace, power and exceptional versatility. In 2011 the Slate family was one of 50 winning entries chosen for inclusion in the ATypI Letter.2 competition in Buenos Aires.

Type+Design: www.beautifuloutlaw.com

Colophon

Distributed in Canada by the Literary Press Group: www.lpg.ca
Distributed in the USA by Small Press Distribution: www.spdbooks.org
Shop on-line at www.bookthug.ca

BOOK
PRODUCTION
WAR ECONOMY
STANDARD

16 17 18 19 20 · 5 4 3 2 1